THE

FOODIST

BUCKET

LIST

100 Edible Adventures
from Farm to Fork

Iver Marjerison

FoodFlow

Publications

Inquiries: Marjerison@gmail.com

Heroic editing & photography by: Kelsey Vlamis (IG: @TheHungryThinker)

"One cannot think well, love well,
sleep well, if one has not dined well"
— Virginia Woolf,
A Room of One's Own

Table of Contents

Upcountry Maui...91

East Maui.. 123

Names & Notes 130
One Last Thing… 131

Local Lingo

Da Kine (duh-kai-n):
Popular slang functioning as a placeholder name, the word is used to refer to objects, people, or places instead of their actual name. Extremely variable in its usage, it can refer to a specific person or abstract concept.
Ex: "Are you still eating at da kine today?"

Grindz (grinez):
Culinary slang referring to food, especially local. Ex: "The Foodist Bucket List is packed with the best island grindz."

'Ono (ō-, nō):
Hawaiian for delicious, or pleasing to the senses in terms of food and drink. The word can be used twice to intensify meaning.
Ex: "The eats in that Foodist book are 'ono 'ono!"

Braddah (brah-dah):
Local Hawaiian slang for "bro".
Ex: "Have you seen that awesome Bucket List book, braddah?"

Shaka (shah-kah):
Internationally recognized Hawaiian hand gesture, made by extending the thumb and pinky while closing the three middle fingers. Acts as a greeting and used to convey the "Aloha Spirit".
Ex: "You cut that guy off! Throw a shaka to apologize."

About Maui

Millions of years ago two massive volcanoes sitting adjacent to each other in the Pacific Ocean simultaneously erupted. The resulting lava flow filled in the area between them and, as it cooled, formed the landmass that we know today as the island of Maui.

Around 400-600 CE, Polynesians traversed 2000+ miles in canoes to settle the area. Slowly, these people established the kingdom and culture of Hawaii. They remained sovereign for some 1500 years, but after British explorer James Cook discovered the Hawaiian islands in 1778, the Western world set its sights on their natural resources and strategic positioning.

Eventually, American businessmen established themselves as political leaders and land owners, gradually undermining the power of the Hawaiian Kingdom's rule. Things came to a head in 1893, when a coup of armed local white men (with the backing of 162 US Marines) overthrew Queen Liliʻuokalani, the last sovereign monarch of the Kingdom of Hawaii.

The "Republic of Hawaii" came to power, with Sanford Dole (yes, that Dole, of the pineapple tycoon family) as president. Eager for the protection and approval of the US, the new republic immediately asked the US government to annex it. Initially many people, including US President Grover Cleveland, questioned the lawless overthrow of a peaceful allied nation's government and were skeptical about siding with the treasonous usupers.

But soon a new president came into office, and in 1900 Hawaii was officially made a territory of the US and would go on to become the 50th state in 1959. In 1993, US Congress passed the Apology Resolution, which acknowledged that "the Native Hawaiian people never directly relinquished to the United States their claims to their inherent sovereignty as a people over their national lands."

To this day, some consider Hawaii a sovereign nation that is illegally occupied by the US.

About Regions

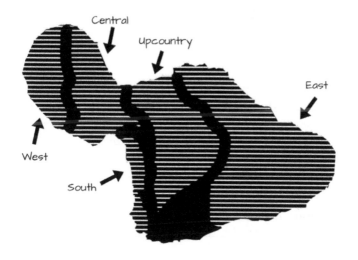

The island of Maui is divided into five distinct regions: West, Central, South, Upcountry, and East. Each of these areas hosts their own delicious variety of places to eat, farms to visit, and edible adventures to be had! To maximize the convenience of the book's food themed quests, it has been divided into five sections accordingly. **The list order is completely random**, so feel free to cross off items one region at a time, or skip around to fit your fancy.

About the List

1. Not All Inclusive

No, I didn't eat everywhere...

This list is not an unbiased ranking of every dish in town, nor does it try to be. *My method is simple: I ask, read, research, and scour the area for the ultimate edible adventures (generally leaning toward less expensive and unique items). I then try them out, and whichever ones spin my head around, go in the book!*

Please note: The items are listed randomly; the page numbers are not "ranks" but merely for reference purposes.

2. Inconsistencies

The food and beverage industry is inherently volatile. Certain dishes come and go, chefs have bad days, and with an island that relies heavily on the seasonal labor of often distracted younger generations... lackluster service is capable of striking at any moment. If I lead you somewhere that lets you down, I apologize in advance.

3. Adventure

This list intends to introduce you to a wide array of experiences that define Maui's unique cuisine. While I list specific items, I strongly encourage personalization and improvisation—you know what you like! Think of this like a food-driven scavenger hunt that you can (and should) tailor to your own desires.

4. No Paid Endorsements

All 100 items in this book are things that I have personally indulged in, and found to be fantastically-awesome.

**None of the items have made the list
due to financial compensation of any kind.**

5. No Addresses or Color?!

The two questions I get the most, both of which have simple answers. First: You have a smartphone and the name of the restaurant—get creative. Second: obviously color photos would look better, but the book would cost a left arm more. You want to pay a left arm more? Didn't think so. Want color? Go follow me on my Instagram: @MauiFoodist, or go see them for yourself!

6. Satisfaction

Whether you seek out every adventure, successfully filling each page's box with a fat check mark, or only take the journeys in your mind from the comfort of your favorite chair, this book should leave you (and your stomach) with a sense of satisfaction.

**If for some reason it doesn't meet these expectations,
let me know. I'm always looking to improve.**

Marjerison@Gmail.com

THE
FOODIST
BUCKET
LIST

West Maui

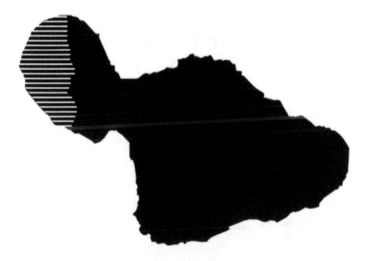

Once used as a retreat for Hawaiian royalty, the northwest coast is known for its abundant sunshine and world-famous sunsets. Whether you're exploring the historic whaling town of Lahaina, enjoying the pristine resorts of Kaanapali, or just traversing the mountainside, this area offers a mess of edible quests to embark upon.

1
Choice Health Bar
Dessert Sunrise
Acai Bowl

These bowls are essentially a blend of yogurt toppings, smoothie fruits, and the Brazilian Acai Palm's nutrient- packed purple berries. Thanks to its recent popularity, cheap imitations—heavy on fruit juice, low on Acai—have become widespread. Luckily, the island has this place to do it right: pure Acai blended with Maui-grown mac nut milk and local honey, topped with a flavor party of granola and fresh fruit. Be sure to opt for the "Make it Epic" topping, and wash it down with a shot of noni juice.

2
Coconut Caboose
Coconut
Coconut Water

At the end of the day, I'm the last guy who wants to pay for something that is literally growing on trees all around me, but when I do, I go for a quality experience like this! These guys are conveniently located (with easy parking), their coconuts are always ice-cold, and they serve up a range of other coconut deliciousness (the ice cream is not to be missed!)

... what else could you ask for?

3
Ululani's Shaved Ice
Pickled Mango
Local Motion

As Maui's most awarded shaved ice joint, the absurd amount of different flavors and unique add-ons offered here are known to stress out even the most confident frozen-sugar connoisseurs. Stay calm though... I got you covered. Go for the Local Motion—but, substitute the boring plain-old mango for the pickled version, and be sure to generously sprinkle the whole thing with their complimentary Li Hing Mui, a confusingly- enticing salted plum powder.

4
Hawaii Fludge Company Lava Flow Fudge

While strolling Lahaina's Front Street, partaking in a handcrafted treat from this local fudgery is all but required. In order to fully saturate yourself in aloha- inspired fudge euphoria, get your hands on the Lava Flow—featuring a combination of milk chocolate and vanilla fudge, sweetened with local Hawaiian sugar cane, and infused with dark roasted Kona coffee.

5
Betty's Beach Cafe
Maine Lobster
Special

This time-honored restaurant offers a diverse menu of things that I... know nothing about. However! I can say that this Wednesday night special is good eating at a <u>crazy</u> cheap price. Combine this Kona-sourced lobster with the oceanfront sunset, and you have all the necessary ingredients for a great Lahaina dinner. Best of all—if timed accordingly—you can get a free view of the Luau next door while you feast!

6
Cane & Canoe
Baked Hawaii

In his original audition tape for the Food Network, Guy Fieri made a sushi roll with pork and french fries. His message was clear: there are no rules. Both metaphorically and literally, this story has always spoken to me, particularly when I have a dish like this, that takes a traditional framework like the Baked Alaska (ice cream, cake, browned meringue) and brings it to a whole new level with tropical flavors and an absolutely adorable presentation.

7
Leoda's Kitchen
Banana Cream
Pie

Located just outside Lahaina inside a seemingly simple plantation-era building, this diner serves up some of the most extraordinarily-flavorsome baked goods on the island. Case in point... this from-scratch pie that combines the tropical sweetness of Maui-grown bananas with a rich and creamy texture that's fit for royalty—truly a fist-fight-over-the-last-bite kind of dessert.

8
Java Jazz
Famous Huevos Rancheros

An eccentric eatery with a lively atmosphere, this is the perfect spot to... well... it's perfect for a lot of things actually, as it's simultaneously a live music venue, bar restaurant, and coffee shop—attached to a boutique, bakery, shaved ice bar, and recording studio. Edibly speaking, everything coming out of this place's kitchen is on point, but their famed huevos are simply unmatched. And for those who prefer to walk on the competitive side of life, they also feature a 50oz in 8- minutes burger challenge.

9
Frida's Mexican Beach House Cactus Fries

After already establishing several successful restaurants in the area, chef owner Mark Ellman opened this oceanfront joint serving a unique fusion menu of eclectic Latin-American dishes, with a twist of Maui- inspired flavors. While even a simple plate of tacos at this spot becomes a taste-bud-fiesta, this novel fried creation is the must-try. If you're asking... I pair mine with the hypnotizing aromatic flavors of their hibiscus lemonade.

10
Star Noodle
From Scratch
Pad Thai

This spot first caught my stomach's eye when I heard that they made their own noodles in-house from scratch... which blew my culinary mind—to be honest, I assumed noodles just came straight from the mystic spaghetti tree—so naturally, I had to check it out. However, it wasn't until after gluttonously stuffing myself with their every-bit-deserving famous Pad Thai, that I was told the rice noodles in this particular dish... are from Thailand.

11
Fleetwood's
$1
Oyster Hour

Located on Lahaina Front Street's prime real estate, this restaurant serves high class eats with prices to match. While you can't go wrong partaking in any of their menu's heroically crafted dishes, I've found that kicking back, enjoying their ocean view, and slurping down oysters for a buck-a-pop, is a great way to foster a beautifully satisfying state of food-induced happiness... without having to liquidate your assets.

12
All The Best...
Poke
Bowls!

Dozens of places serve up these delicious raw fish bowls, so I've narrowed it down to my 3 must-tries:

- *Tamura's — This liquor store has dozens of varieties with unbeatable prices.*
- *Like Poke — A humble food truck serving up the freshest of the fresh!*
- *South Maui Fish Co. — An explosion of crave-worthy freshness and quality in every bite!*

13
Mala Ocean Tavern
Stir-Fried
Brussel Sprouts

Being an enthusiast of variety, I hate to have the same chef featured three times—but in this case—each of his restaurants achieve herculean-levels of deliciousness in such different styles, that I decided it doesn't count. For this eatery, Mark and his team are all about small plates with complexly crafted flavors, like these stir- fried Brussels sprouts with their charred outer layer complemented by refreshing mint.

14
Down the Hatch
Lava Lava Shrimp

Friend, you are on a culinary quest. A quest for novelty. A quest for the extraordinary. A quest for all that is true. This dish, friend, will prove a pivotal moment in your quest. However long the line is, wait in it. Whatever price they ask, pay it. If a monstrous beast blocks your path, slay it. Hear me when I tell you, these fried shrimp with "lava lava sauce" will take you wherever you need to go... just ask Guy Fieri.

15
Honu Seafood & Pizza
Award-Winning
Ahi Bruschetta

I could tell you about the outlandish freshness of the delicately-seared ahi, romanticize the meaty-flesh of the local tomatoes, bore you with analogies for the aged-balsamic's complex flavor profile, or fill a page describing the way the flaxseed bread seamlessly melds the entire creation together... but really, any dish that wins the revered "Best of the Fest" award, speaks for itself.

76
Gazebo
Famous
Fried Rice

If you spend any length of time on the island you are sure to hear rumors of this ridiculously sized mountain of rice—and for good reason. The absurd amount of savory breakfast-brilliance that this dish packs comes from the synergistic medley of veggies and diced Portuguese sausage, fried beautifully with rice, and topped with fluffy eggs. Word of the wise, avoid the notoriously long lines by ordering it to go.

17
Island Cream Co.
Mini Sampler

I hate places like this... their beautiful display of overwhelming flavors, the bright colors, happy people, and local ingredients, all flaunted in your face. It's like they want to make sure that, no matter what flavor you choose, you will always wish you had gotten to enjoy more. It's a viciously flirtatious game of frozen ecstasy, which I never seem to win.

...WAIT! They let you get 6 different flavors!?
...In one dish?!
...I love places like this.

78
Maui Dragon Fruit
Farm Fresh Dragon Fruit

Nestled in the hillside overlooking Lahaina sits the island's only farm dedicated to producing the exotic dragon fruit. If your taste buds haven't yet experienced these fruits, they pack a richly sweet flavor with the perfect melt-in-your-mouth texture, best enjoyed by the spoonful. While it's fun enough to nosh on fresh fruit and enjoy the spectacular view, this adventure gets even better thanks to their daily tours, zip-lining, and aqua-ball rides.

79
Pacific'O Restaurant
Kula Beets

On the surface, they have all the regular fixings of a high-end Maui restaurant: romantic oceanfront view, a wait staff exhibiting machine-like professionalism, and Food Network caliber chefs. However, there is one thing that radically sets this joint apart—they have their very own upcountry farm*, supplying them with a daily supply of produce. A particularly drool-worthy result of their "farm-to-chef" approach is this plate, which varies in preparation and accompanying flavors depending on the season.

*Featured as item #90

20
Slappy Cakes
Do-It Yourself

I know, I know—you love to eat out for breakfast, but you hate letting someone else play with the pancake batter. Well, I have good news... This place combines the atmosphere and ingredients of your favorite breaky-joint, with a built-in-the-table griddle to fry your own cakes! Best of all, the batter comes in a squeeze bottle with a nozzle for precision 'caking, making it the ultimate place to flex your culinary creativity.

21
Maui Prime Fine Foods
DIY Cheese Tray

Of course, a large part of immersing yourself in a cuisine is letting the local chefs work their magic for you. However, I also believe a quintessential part of fully experiencing an area's food, requires getting a little hands on. If you agree, this store—full of cured meats, artisanal cheeses, and other gourmet goodies— has everything you need. To maximize the potential awesomeness, I suggest pairing their cheeses with some local fruit and a bottle of wine... and enjoying it on the local beach, picnic style.

22
Merriman's
Sunset Glass of Wine

Yes... Front Street's ice cream shops are great, and the restaurants are top-notch—but when it comes to the ultimate edible Lahaina adventure, it's all about where you watch that world-renowned sunset. The best spot is highly debated, but posting up at this open-seating bar, sipping a glass of bone-dry wine, and noshing on their seasonal cheese plate—is my personal favorite. Time it right and you can get your drink ordered just as happy hour ends, slowly savor some eats, then kick back and enjoy the show.

Central Maui

This area is littered with Maui's usual suspects: abundant beach activities and a head-spinning assortment of shopping. However, it's also home to much of the island's local community, so while they still offer the expected tourist- focused dining options, there is also a range of off-the-beaten-path spots serving up eats with a more "local" feel.

23
Esters Fair Prospect
Classic Daiquiri

A great cocktail is hard to find. A great cocktail served by a knowledgeable and passionate, yet not pretentious or condescending, bartender? Harder yet. All of the above at an affordable price? Unheard of ... until I found this little slice of heaven on Wailuku's Main Street. Bring old friends for a few rounds, or go belly up to the bar and make new ones. Order your favorite cocktail, or let the bartender surprise you. Happy hour, or a nightcap. With this bar, there are no wrong choices.

24
Donut Dynamite
Maui Vanilla Bean Brioche Donut

This husband and wife team crank out the best donuts ~~on the island~~ I have ever had the pleasure of devouring. They take extreme pride in their gourmet process—hand crafting them in small batches each day and using fruits from friend's gardens. They even take "from-scratch" literally, making their own version of Oreo's and Graham Crackers to crush as toppings. It's hard to really portray my enthusiasm without being able to grab you by the shoulders and yell, nonetheless... GO HERE!

25
Julia's
Best Banana Bread

After an hour of winding up and down switchbacks, hugging guard rails, and squeezing down the notoriously less-than-one-lane road, you find yourself at this famed little green shack. Now, I can't say for sure what makes this bread* so delicious—I like to think it's a secret family recipe passed down through generations—but it's possible it's just due to the celebratory appetite that gets worked up from surviving the drive...

*Smearing with lilikoi butter <u>highly</u> recommended.

26
Brigit & Bernard's
Zueri Gschnetzlets
(Bernard's Hometown Special)

With huge portions of traditional German dishes*— cooked by
Bernard and served by Brigit—it's hard to get any more authentic
than this place. While I could talk all day about this mess of tender
meat smothered in rich sauce, the rest of their brilliantly crafted
menu, or even their enormous Eastern European beer selection, you
really just need to do your inner meat- lover a favor and check this
place out for yourself.

*Vegetarians beware

27
Maui Fresh Streatery
Cuisine-Inspired
Basket of Fries

Refusing to play by the typical food truck rules, Chef Kyle has instead embraced a deliciously novel idea: source seasonal and represent global. This means his menu is always changing—relying on the flavors and ingredients locally in season—to showcase one specific cuisine at a time. While he celebrates the variability of his ever-rotating menu, he always features this crowd- pleasing basket of fries—inspired by the currently embraced cuisine, and infused with the island's flavors- of-the-season.

Call or check online for current location!

28
Geste Shrimp
Spicy Pineapple
Shrimp Plate

While I have no evidence to support this, it is my belief that the flavor gurus behind this food truck (usually parked by Kahului Harbor) are also master shrimp fishermen. It's simply the only explanation fo``r how they can have such a consistent supply of succulently-massive shrimp. Nonetheless, everyday people are deterred by the questionable condition of their van, opting for one of the more high-tech looking trucks parked nearby... <u>don't</u> be one of these people.

29
Home Maid Bakery
Cream Filled
Malasada

"Malasada is a Portuguese confection, made of egg-sized balls of yeast dough that are deep-fried and coated with sugar."
-Wikipedia

"Malasada is an edible orb of cloud-like fluffiness, filled with an intoxicating concoction of creamy sweetness, that create an unfathomable melt-in-your-mouth dessert experience."

-Me

30
Poi By The Pound
Laulau Plate

This traditional Hawaiian food preparation consists of slow cooking meat that's been wrapped in taro leaves until it becomes ridiculously tender. While this dish is served all over the island, these guys are a local favorite—known for their traditionally crafted mouth- watering flavors. Plus, they serve it with a heaping bowl of their own "poi"—a paste consisting of mashed taro root—which I personally find to be oddly irresistible... despite its lack of any distinguishable taste.

37
Tasaka
Pineapple Guri- Guri

Alright, fine... so maybe food romance isn't the best way to describe a Dixie-cup served treat. Regardless, this family owned hole-in-the-wall serves up a uniquely tasty homemade cross between sherbet and ice cream, a hybridized frozen dessert known as "Guri-guri".

32
Maui Coffee Roaster Cappy Hour

Maui's oldest coffee roaster specializes in serving up a variety of handcrafted pastries, delectable eats for breakfast and lunch, and of course, a range of locally sourced Hawaiian-style coffee drinks. These delicious flavors are beautifully complimented by the hip café vibe, with walls featuring local art and a near-tangible buzz of enthusiastic energy. While I could have filled a dozen list items with their assortment of perfect pours, their cappuccino-themed happy hour is the caffeine experience to go out of your way for.

33
Fork & Salad
Salad Creation!

If you think creating the perfect salad is an art, then these guys will be your new favorite studio. Boasting a massive selection of the best salad toppings, fresh local greens, and homemade dressings, this spot is the perfect place to get your veggie fix. They have plenty of specialties, but if you're the salad artist that I know you are, you gotta go DIY!

34
Ichiban Okazuya
Local Style
Plate Lunch

These guys crank out truly local style food, in flavorful heaping portions, for near-robbery prices. To be clear, I'm referring to the food that locals actually eat—like slow cooked meats, mac-salad, and piles of white rice—not the more-glamorized "Hawaiian" foods like smoothies and poke bowls. While they have a variety of plate lunches that will provide a deliciously authentic experience, I personally opt for the Chicken Katsu.

35
Wow-Wee Maui
Traditional Kava Bowl

This cloudy brown drink, made from the mashing of kava roots, is quite popular in Pacific Ocean cultures, and often consumed in ritualistic settings. However, it should be noted that the drink has not gained fame for tasting like candy. Rather, the popularity of this earthy-flavored and confusingly bitter drink comes from its sedative properties, said to help foster a state of relaxation without clouding mental clarity.

36
Kumu Farms
From-The-Tree Papaya

Located a rock's throw from a papaya orchard, this quaint farm stand offers a daily assortment of just- harvested fruits and veggies, including their famed strawberry sunrise papaya. After you nosh a half dozen of these buttery-sweet fruits, head across the street to the historic Maui Tropical Plantation. This massive agricultural fanta-syland features zip-lines, gift shops, a restaurant, a soap factory, and even a tram tour of the farm!

37
Four Sisters Bakery
Butter Rolls

The Crafting of these lusted-over pastries was once an art, a delicate process that required meticulous ingredient ratios, and skillful preparation. Over the years, driven by convenience and cost, people began to take short cuts. Technological advances eroded the traditional methods, and they soon became nothing more than oily globs of doughy salt. Naturally, I set out on a quest for someone who stayed true, and after trying dozens of spots, on the verge of giving up, I found these rolls... with each bite embodying the authentic fusion of fluffy and rich savory perfection.

38
A Saigon Cafe
Vietnamese Crepe

This authentic Vietnamese eatery is a hidden gem, literally—you would never find it if you weren't looking. However, despite their seemingly nonexistent attempt at modern business marketing, the joint has a lively contemporary vibe with a casual wait staff known for cracking jokes. Their plate-to-smash is this Asian style crepe, combining a rice flour and coconut milk base with a flavor-punch of veggies, meats, and spices, served with a fist full of greens... that I swear they just grabbed from the backyard.

39
Sam Sato's
Dry Mein

This old-school family-run eatery has been serving up locally be-loved comfort food since Sam Sato first opened doors in 1933. Most famous of which is this featured noodle dish, consisting of a simple combination of perfectly al dente noodles, bits of diced pork, chopped green onions, and of course, the family- guarded super-top-secret noodle seasoning. The resulting unforgettable bowl of satisfy-ing-savory- perfection will have even the most devoted gluten-avoiding carb-haters begging for more. *CASH ONLY!*

40
Alive & Well
Maui Gold Smoothie

This health food market offers an impressive range of natural beauty products, supplements, fresh produce, and other grocery items, but the real story is their café. Frequented by locals of all ages and life-styles, they offer a mess of fresh juices, simple and healthy grab-and-go meals, and of course, foodie-acclaimed smoothies. While it's hard to go wrong when they're running the blender, with this trio of local fruit, it's like your drinking the island.

47
808 on Main
Peanut Butter
Chocolate S'more

Few things in life compare to this beloved campfire treat. The perfectly gooey 'mallow, the velvety warm chocolate, and the satisfying crunch... combining to sing a symphony of nostalgia inducing deliciousness. However—for some bizarre reason—most restaurants sadly refuse to celebrate this epic flavor-trio. Lucky for Maui, we have these dessert-innovators, willing to break the status quo to give the people what they want! They even go a step further by ingeniously adding chocolates best friend into the mix... peanut butter!

42
Maui Specialty Chocolates
Dark Chocolate
Truffle Mochi

Grab a glass of milk, put on your dessert-eating pants, and prepare to embark on an unforgettable flavor journey into the mochi world of gooey-chocolaty perfection. These amusingly squishy patties consist of a jelly-like outer layer, made from a special variety of glutinous rice flour, and are stuffed with the richly bittersweet taste of dark chocolate ganache. The novel texture creates an oddly enjoyable mouth feel that is sure to leave your sweet tooth curiously satisfied.

43
Acevedo's Hawaicano
Carne Asada Fries

Dear Creator of Carne Asada Fries,

THANK YOU!!!!!!!!!!!!!!!!!!!!!!!!!!!!!!!!!!

Sincerely,
Iver's Taste Buds

44
Tasty Crust
World Famous Pancakes

An iconic Maui landmark, this no-frills diner serves up generous plates of all your favorite breakfast comfort foods. The most famous being their award-winning pile of deliciously fluffy pancakes. While I admit it has little to do with tropical flavors, or the aloha spirit, there is just something about the heaping portion size, the artery-clogging slab of butter, and the obligatory drenching of syrup that will always hold a special place in my stomach's heart.

45
Auntie Lia's Baked Goods Lilikoi Bread

When it comes to Maui's baked good scene, it seems everyone and their mothers are making the same old banana bread. Now, don't get me wrong, I'm just as likely to be found hiding in a tree-fort gorging insatiably on banana bread as the next guy... but there is something refreshing about unique fruit breads— like lilikoi! While I can't say if Lia* invented it or not, I can say it's the best I have yet to find—and believe me, I've looked.

*Her cart can usually be found at the Maui Swap Meet

46
Umi
Soft Shell Crab Bau Buns

This is a Wailuku staple and a guaranteed spot for a quality eats. Now normally, I'm the kind of guy who reads the Google description and says, come on, we can do better. But honestly, for this spot — "Quaint Japanese joint serving sushi, sashimi, steak & seafood in a pared-down locale" — I gotta tip my hat. They nailed it. But I would add: "PLUS INCREDIBLE BAU BUNS THAT ARE SO FUN AND DELICIOUS THAT THEY MAKE YOUR SOUL SMILE!"

South Maui

This stretch of the island is known for its loads of sunshine, lack of rain, and miles of paradise- esque beaches. It is also home to some of Maui's finest high-end resorts. As such, the usual food buzz tends to be about the prestigious white- table-cloth sort of experiences—the majority of which, to be fair, tend to do a consistently mouth-watering job. However, don't get star- struck, they are far from the extent of the area's deliciously-edible potential.

47
Shaka Pizza
White Spinach Pizza

It may seem culinarily absurd for me to condone noshing a slice of pizza when surrounded by such an abundant supply of higher caliber eats, but sometimes you just gotta keep it simple. If you're looking for a quick-and-easy meal that is affordable and still satisfyingly delicious... a slice of this locally loved New York style pizza can't be beat!

48
'Ami 'Ami Bar & Grill
Peanut Butter
Belgium Waffle

- ☐ 1 Full – Deep Fried Belgium Waffle
- ☐ 3 Scoops (heaping) – Chocolate Ice Cream
- ☐ 2 Dollops – Fresh Whipped Cream
- ☐ 1 (sliced) – Local Strawberry
- ☐ 1 Handful (chopped) – Roasted Peanuts

Drizzle generously with peanut butter and chocolate sauce, disregard manners, and devour with reckless abandon.

49
Yee's Orchard
Golden Glow Mango

Grown exclusively on Yee's farm, this famous variety of mango is known around the islands for its candy-like sweetness and buttery texture. Though the mangoes can be seen in a handful of grocery stores, its best to go right to the source! Yee's farm stand sits in front of his orchard, just outside of Kihei, and is open daily.

50
Kihei Caffe
Banana Mac Nut
French Toast

The regular adjectives and wordy descriptions just don't seem to do this dish justice—instead, let me tell it in a story: imagine if the richness of fried eggs were to marry the fluffy-deliciousness of sliced white bread. Together, they had a kid that got his PhD in banana-tastic-ness, and married the satisfying crunch of roasted macadamia nuts. They too, then had a kid of their own... this plate, piled with all of the best things in life, would be that kid.

51
Wow Wow
Hawaiian Lemonade
Lilikoi with
Strawberry Float

This fully customizable lemonade bar sources local sugar cane and fruits, and is awesome to the point that it warrants a sports analogy! Now, I'm not huge on these, but if I were, I would probably say something witty and clever like...

> *"This place is the grand-slam hole-in-one, slam-dunk double-turkey, hat-trick royal-flush, MVP... of the lemonade world."*

52
Ko
Ahi On The Rock

One thing that becomes quickly apparent when eating your way across the island is the abundance of ahi. From sushi and poke to tacos and salads, Hawaii's cuisine celebrates the rich taste of this locally caught fish in nearly every form. As such, it's rare to find an ahi-centric meal that hasn't been done a thousand times before. One delicious exception is this dish by Chef Tylun Pang that features fat chunks of raw fish, ginger miso sauce, and a boiling hot rock to "sear-it-yourself."

53
Eskimo Candy
World Famous
Seafood Chowder

This place is exactly like your local deli, full of grab- and-go meals that allow you to pick up a quick lunch at an affordable price. Only difference is... instead of bologna sandwiches and chips—they serve grilled fish and poke. Instead of chicken noodle soup—they serve fresh-caught seafood chowder. And instead of some underwhelming painting—there is massive jaw-open shark shooting out of the wall.

54
Roasted Chiles
Roasted Jalapeno
Margarita

1. Food bursting with the spicy-flavor awesomeness that can only come from handcrafted family recipes.
2. More types of tequila than you can shake a stick at.
3. A margarita that features fresh-squeezed lime juice and pulverized roasted jalapeños, lightly sweetened with pure agave syrup.

...Check, Check, and Check!

55
Coconut's Fish Cafe Fish Tacos with Mango Salsa

There's definitely a reason this place has served over a million people... why their online presence is search- engine clogging... and why there is always an absurdly long line. It's probably the way the wasabi melds with the tangy sweetness of the mango salsa—or maybe it's the savory medley of grilled mahi mahi and ono— actually, I bet it's the way each corn tortilla is so generously stacked with heaping portions...

Alright, I give up... just go taste for yourself!

56
Fabiani's
Lilikoi Macaron

This unique confectionary features two meringue- based cookies sandwiched around a sweet and creamy ganache-style filling. The trick is, the egg white and almond flour-based cookies must be baked with near science-experiment precision in order to rise properly. This creates the celebrated rippled edge, known as the "foot," along with the melt-in-your-mouth texture. Point is, properly crafted macarons are a true culinary treasure... and when you have your first bite, you'll see why!

57
Maui Fish'n Chips
Fish & Chips

When you go to a psychic, they ask you about your back pain or car trouble—because everyone has them.

When I talk about food you need to try, I mention this spot—because everyone loves good fish and chips.

Pay the extra couple buck$ for the mahi-mahi, and (obviously) get the loaded garlic fries.

58
Sugar Beach Bake Shop
Lilikoi Key Lime Pie

Alright, so I should start by saying that for this particular item, I am a bit biased. I happen to become helpless in the presence of creamy-textured desserts, I get completely overwhelmed by the zesty citrus flavors of fresh lime, I'm a sucker for anything boasting the fruity-sweetness of local lilikoi, and when these factors become compounded into one fresh-baked treat? I become utterly incapable of rational judgment. With that being said... I-LOVE-THIS-PIE! ! ! ! !

59
Matteo's Osteria
Wine On-Tap

"I only want a glass or two, but hate having my choices limited to their handful of pre-opened bottles…"

<u>If you or a loved one has ever experienced the above situation, than you may be one of the millions of wine enthusiasts who struggle with, "by-the-glass-dysphoria."</u>

Fortunately, there is an answer—Matteo's wine bar, featuring an entire wall of different wines preserved by their state-of-the-art tap system. Taste, sample, mix, and match glasses to your indecisive heart's content!

60
Cinnamon Roll Fair
Macadamia Nut
Cinnamon Roll

Some call it an edible blunder, others a culinary disgrace,
That we've allowed our beloved cinni' to be so sadly replaced.

A pastry that once celebrated the perfection of gooey-richness,
Has turned into scantly dressed loaves of depressing fluffiness.

But this place holds true, and with your first bite you'll see, They serve
these baked goodies the way they were meant to be.

61
Maui Bread Company
Baked Ube Mochi

Just your warm and friendly local bakery that uses the highest quality ingredients, and bakes each of their morsels of heaven with a healthy dose of love. From savory baked goods to the obligatory banana bread, these guys have it all! Personally, I dig the sweet potato mochi—it's baked instead of steamed, and it's a handy on-the-go snack. But my real suggestion? Don't take suggestions! This one is simple: walk inside, follow your nose, and grab a coconut coffee to wash it down.

62
Sansei
50% Off Sushi Special

When seeking Maui's best eats—fish truly is king
And we all know rolling it in rice makes the flavors sing

Luckily for us, there is sushi served on every block
With creative rolls and fresh fish that truly rock

But with so many tasty options how can one be the best?
How about a half-off special to separate from the rest!

63
Monkeypod Kitchen Famous Mai Tai

When it comes to the drink market on tropical islands, there is one thing guaranteed—an oversaturation of places serving up "the best Mai Tai." So I set out to see which of these claims held true, and was about to declare a 213-way tie when I came across this version. Truly a work of mixology art; the drink features Lahaina dark and light rum layered with flavors of lime, orange, and mac nut, and is finished off with their secret weapon... honeyed lilikoi foam.

64
Cafe O' Lei
Baked Maui Onion Soup

My appreciation for this spot stems from their seamless combination of high-quality dishes and refreshingly casual atmosphere. However, my infatuation for this spot is fostered by the robust flavor symphony of this seemingly simple soup—and the Christmas-morning- like warmness that permeates my soul with each taste of the delicate pastry shell, the savory broth, the sweet Maui onions, and richness of gruyere cheese.

Yes… it's that good.

65
Maui Brewing Company
Fresh Brewed
Coconut Porter

Just inland from Kihei is a beer-lovers paradise where the taps flow freely while live music and laughter fill the air. This contagious positive energy makes it the perfect place to kill a few hours playing life sized- Jenga, touring the brew-house, and enjoying good company. All, of course, while sipping on this ice-cold glass of tropically sweet Maui-grown flavors.

66
Three's Bar and Grill
Kula Pork Nachos

This savory-flavor project rocks a trio of homemade chips, layered with sweet and juicy slow-cooked Kalua pork, smothered in a zesty basil guacamole and pepper jack, drizzled with truffle lime aioli, and sprinkled with diced tomatoes. Top all this with a 50% off deal, their equally awesome drink specials, a regular supply of live music, and a comfortable patio… and you have my go-to option for Kihei happy hour.

Upcountry Maui

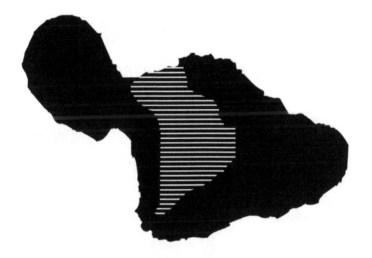

This area starts on the North Shore with the historic coastal town of Paia, and stretches south, climbing windy roads through the majestic mountainside. The area's fertile volcanoic soils and growing climate have long made it a chef-celebrated source for the finest tropical ingredients, and are responsible for the rich agricultural scene that can be experienced first hand via the abundance of roadside produce stands and on-farm adventures.

67
Mana Foods
Island-Renowned
Produce Section

Since 1983, this store has evolved from an unassuming local shop into an award winning and highly revered health food super store—with shelves full of natural beauty, health, and food products of all kinds. Thanks to their sourcing from over 400 local vendors, their produce section is overflowing with Maui-grown fruits and veggies, making it the ultimate way to get lost for a few hours: skipping, laughing, and smiling in a dazzling state of fresh-food-loving bliss.

68
Cafe Mambo
Kalua Duck Quesadilla

This flavor bomb starts by generously layering honeyed Kalua duck—slow cooked to juicy perfection and fork- pulled into tender shreds—on top a monster-sized flour tortilla. It's then dressed with shredded cheese and caramelized onions, griddle toasted, and cut into just-able-to-be-held triangles. The overwhelming meaty-gooey-awesomeness is sure to leave you licking fingers and questioning why chicken is even an option.

69
Paia Fish Market
Fish Taco Plate

Since '89 this iconic eatery has specialized in serving up heaping plates of quality seafood with a reasonable price tag—and based solely on the length of their daily lunch line, it's safe to assume they do a darn good job. Be warned, this dish isn't for those diners afraid of getting messy. Be prepared to toss the fork, tuck your napkin, and dig in to these scrumptiously overloaded tacos, fingers first!

70
Café Des Amis
Bacon & Avocado Crepe

Based on a hunger-inducing fusion of French and Indian cuisines, their menu features both perfectly spiced curries and an assortment of flavorsome crepes—what more could you ask for? While both sweet and savory options hit a masterful level of crepe- wizardry, this item steals the show, combining the creaminess of island-picked avocados with bacon's beloved umami-slap, and an oddly delicious twist of delicately sweet apple chunks.

77
Paia Gelato
Lilikoi Quark...
In a Waffle Cone

Maui's gross oversaturation of the frozen dessert market can be a bit overwhelming to say the least. I've witnessed some of the pickiest eaters get flustered by the variety of choices and end up licking a poorly creamed cone of boring old vanilla. To avoid a similar fate, I recommend seeking out this shop, consistently scooping epically delectable treats in a variety of both classic and locally inspired flavors—like this infusion that uses goat cheese from the farm up the road.

72
Mama's Fish House Restaurant
Polynesian Black Pearl

A list of Maui's edible adventures could never be complete without mention of this world-renowned beachfront restaurant. While the ridiculous amount of awards won by this place may seem overblown, the unblemished love of the atmosphere and food—by locals and tourists alike—speaks for itself. Although dinner at this spot is obviously great, I've found that sitting at the bar, watching the sunset, and partaking in this famous chocolate-clad mousse dish is a great way to get a feel for the famed experience—without breaking the pocket book.

Kula Marketplace
Local Treasures

Located on the Kula Highway (just a rocks throw from item #87) sits a simple store, often assumed to be just another knick-knack souvenir shop... but oh how wrong this fatal assumption is! For this marketplace happens to boast one of the most novel collections of food goodies on the entire island. From internationally sourced exotics to local preserves, this shop has been curated to feature edible must-haves for every sort of food lover. Best of all... Spam flavored mac-nuts!

74
Maui Kombucha Bar
Ginger- Spiced Kombucha

Long story short, kombucha is a sparkling black tea beverage, often flavored with fruits, and the result of a fermentation process that uses bacteria and yeast. This process transforms the sugar in the beverage into lactic acid, giving it a slightly tart taste, filling it with healthy pro-biotic bacteria, and creating a tasty soda-like carbonation. It may sound weird, but remember that foods like bread, wine, yogurt, and cheese all rely on a similar chemical process—so there is nothing to be afraid of!

75
Colleen's
Goat Cheese &
Portobello Omelet

Haiku's local breakfast spot serves up the traditional morning fair you'd expect from a small-town diner, with the modern twists you'd expect from a big city bistro. For example, this traditional-but-edgy featured omelet with a load of sautéed mushrooms that create a perfect flavor canvas for the sharpness of the local goat cheese. Beautifully achieving the delicate balance between hearty and healthy, this spot is the perfect way to fuel up for a day of Hawaiian-style adventures.

76
Maui Pineapple Tour
Field-Fresh Pineapple

know what you're thinking...

"Gee wiz, it sure would be cool to
go to a farm and finally see some pineapple..."
...Trees?
...Bushes?
...Vines?

I'm not spoiling it. Go find out for yourself!

77
NUKA
Cucumber Roll
& Asian Fries

On this island you can basically throw a rock and hit three different sushi restaurants serving up fresh-fish- stuffed edible creations. With how convenient it is to find your basic top-notch rolls, I like to seek out those that are truly unique—which is where this place comes in. This artful roll matches the texture and flavor of the usual sushi suspects with the refreshing crunch of cucumber. Pair with their crave-worthy wasabi-spiced fries and you're in for a sushi-filled good time.

78
Hali'imaile General Store
Soshimi Napoleon

Fat layers of raw salmon and tuna, stacked with fried wontons, and drizzled with sesame-soy vinaigrette.

...If that isn't enough to convince you to abandon your responsibilities and pursue this dish,
then we're not friends.

79
Hali'imaile
Distilling Company
Pineapple Vodka Tasting

"Hmm... Sounds awfully sweet and pineapple-y."
I know, right?! I thought the exact same thing!

However, while the process starts with Maui-grown pineapples, thanks to fermentation and their unique state-of-the-art glass-distillation process, it ends with a shockingly smooth intoxicating liquid that shows no sign of its former fruitiness. Still skeptical? Take a tour, shoot a sample, and see for yourself!

80
Paia Bowls
Bulletproof Coffee

Every day some kid on Instagram tries to tell you the "new and improved" way to drink coffee. But you take no heed, for your current coffee method is your forever coffee method. But then, you have your first bulletproof coffee... and your life is changed. Served hot, this drink features clarified butter and coconut oil, blended (with a blender!) to create a perfectly homogenized cup of brain nourishment. Bonus: their acai is life and their patio is a beautiful oasis in the midst of Paia madness.

Maui Chocolate Tour Cacao Tasting

Ahhh... chocolate! Mayan spiritual elixir, sought-after dessert, and nutritional superfood—but how much do we really know? For starters, it does not come from the Hershey's tree. It is made from ground seeds, harvested from the football-shaped fruit of the cacao tree. The transformation into your favorite chocolate bar requires drying, fermenting, grinding, and mixing, each step contributing to the final bar's unique flavors. But why hear about it from me when you can go to a real cacao orchard to taste the experience for yourself!

82
Jaws Country Store
Breakfast Toast

So you're all set for the road to Hana. You've got your guidebook app downloaded, and your #HanaDreamin Spotfiy playlist ready, you know exactly where Coconut Glen's is (#97), and you're up early to beat the tour buses—but wait a second! You just passed through Paia, and you haven't eaten yet. Have no fear! These guys are just another 10 miles up the road. Their kitchen is ready to serve up the breakfast you deserve, and their store has all the provisions needed for your glorious adventure.

83
Upcountry
Farmer's Market
Purple Cosmic Carrots

If you're a fan of fresh produce, then Maui is your spot; the island is littered with farmers markets of all sizes boasting a year-round bounty of fresh flavors to be enjoyed. However, despite the straightforward name, many have become more craft-fair-like, hawking mostly non-edibles. For the true experience... the UFM is the place to be. The deliciously simple difference? They only allow vendors who sell locally grown products—including these purple carrots!

84
T-Komoda Store
& Bakery
Donut On-a-Stick

This legendary upcountry bakery has earned its fame one finger-licking donut at a time... over the course of the last century! The main draw is their ambrosia (Greek mythological word referring to the "food of the gods"... cool right?) status cream puffs—the filling of which redefines creamy custard perfection. However, if you've spent as much time as me in search of a donut experience that doesn't leave your hands a sticky mess for the rest of the week... you know that this featured item is the true masterpiece.

85
Surfing Goat Dairy
Farm-Fresh Cheese Flight

Hangout with goats on the farm...
Eat their cheese off a fork...
...Get it?!

Seriously though... with cheese sampling, goat petting, interactive tours, and hands-on goat milking opportunities, this place really is the definition of a farm-to-fork experience!

Inside tip: bring a bottle of #95 and a picnic blanket!

86
Ocean Vodka Distillery
Maui-Grown Vodka

What do you get when you combine volcanic filtered Hawaiian water and organic sugar cane? Well... not much on its own, but factor in a period of fermentation and distillation—and you have a (really cool looking) bottle of premium Maui vodka. But why explain the details of their field-to-bottle process, when you can go check it out for yourself! This farm/distillery offers daily tours, tastings, and even has a gift shop full of vodka-themed knick-knacks!

87
Kula Lodge
Bloody Mary

Despite the island's delicious abundance of these savory morning beverages, I've decided this one is simply the best. No, they are <u>not</u> using some specialty bacon-infused vodka, they do <u>not</u> serve it with a skewered cheeseburger on the rim, and they are <u>not</u> freshly pulverizing tomatoes... Nope, the true magic of this bloody is all thanks to it being enjoyed on a legendary hillside location and the subsequent snap-as-many-photos-as- you-can view.

88
La Provence
Croissant Aux Amandes

Before the sun has even considered starting his (her?) day, the dessert-gurus at this authentic French bakery have already begun their daily ritual of crafting the island's finest baked goods. These true-to-tradition treats feature exquisite flavor profiles, and the sort of perfect mouth feel that only comes from decades of dedication to the artful craft of pastry making.

Note: this spot is BYOB, and cash only!

89
Kula Bistro
Coconut Shrimp

The world is full of things designed to remain the same—to never evolve. Regular people, like you and me, often accept this and move on with our lives. But then there's the game-changers. The inventor of ride-sharing. The first person to add mayo to a BLT... and the Kula Bistro: the people responsible for taking coconut shrimp to the next level by pairing it with a mound of crispy (and mashed!) purple sweet potatoes.

90
O'o Farm
Farm-to-Plate Lunch

Their daily tour begins with a leisurely stroll through the farm grounds learning about organic agriculture and picking fresh veggies. Next, you gather around an outdoor picnic table to feast on a masterfully crafted lunch featuring the current foods and flavors growing on the farm—that you just got done picking! Finally, the afternoon is finished off sipping on the farm's own grown and roasted coffee while indulging in a seasonally inspired dessert... agritourism at its finest!

97
Ali'1 Kula Lavender
Lavender Coffee & Scone

From soaps to desserts, everything seems to be better when infused with the amazingly aromatic qualities of lavender. Which is why this 13-acre farm, growing 45 different varieties of lavender, and its onsite gift shop selling lavender-based gifts of all kinds, is a truly magical place to be. To fully saturate your senses in this fragrant adventure, get your hands on their infused coffee and scone, kick back overlooking the valley, and get lost in a lavender-scented daydream.

92
Kula Country Farms
You-Pick Strawberries

With putt-putt golf, a produce stand, yard games, you- pick 'berries, and a seasonal corn maize… this place is essentially a food-themed Disneyland—and a must-stop when you're in the upcountry. Be sure to check their social media for special events, or just stop by to stock up on farm-fresh produce. Better yet, bring a blanket and have yourself a fresh fruit picnic while taking in the breath-thieving view of the island.

Grandma's Coffee House Seafood Benedict

Imagine a classic eggs benny... only instead of the boring English muffin, there's a fluffy waffle made from sweet blue corn. Oh, and instead of the tasteless piece of ham, there's a flavorful pile of ocean fresh fish—or crab!

...Died and gone to a brunch-themed heaven? Nope, just another beautiful weekend morning at Grandma's.

94
Ulupalakua Ranch
Grilled Pineapple Elk Burger

Nearly every day of the week this historic ranch-house- turned-grill is packed with a crowd of hungry patrons—and for good reason. Their kitchen and grill consistently crank out a variety of ridiculously tasty eats with the precision of a well-oiled culinary machine. Their specialty being this burger, featuring a freshly ground patty from their own island-raised elk herd, which—when topped with one fatty slice of beautifully charred pineapple—is truly a neglect-loved-ones-until-done kinda burger.

Maui Wine &
Ulupalakua Vineyards
Pineapple Wine

Island's-Only-Winery
Pineapple-Champagne?!
Take-a-Tour
Maui-Grown-Grapes
Locally-Sourced-Pineapples
Aloha-Inspired-Wine
Tropical-Vineyards
Try-a-Sample

96
Baked On Maui
Shakaquila

In a time before our time, the culinary bureaucrats of the world sat down and decided on basic truths: that everything that can be deep-fried should be, that ketchup be a condiment for everything and anything, and that breakfast be a meal be restricted to redundant simplicity. Luckily for us though, there's a revolution in the works, and these guys are the tip of the spear. Leading their charge is this dish—a flavor bomb fusion of shakshuka and chilaquiles.

East Maui

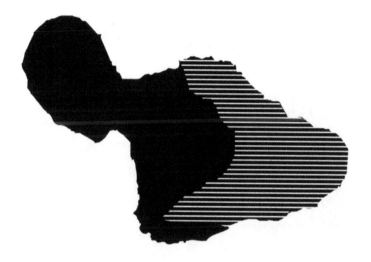

Although technically covering a massive amount of land, the only part of the region that is inhabited enough to be featured in this book is the Hana Highway. This famously jaw- dropping drive, along the waterfall sprinkled coast, cuts through a handful of tropical farms that supply the limited local eateries and various roadside stands with unmatched flavors of aloha-freshness.

97
Coconut Glen's
Coconut Ice Cream

Dear Diary,

This morning 1 set out on the road to Hana in search of the frozen dessert rock star "Coconut Glen." Now to be honest, I've had my dessert- fixated heart broken by fruit based "ice creams" more times than 1 care to admit, so 1 approached this shack with a heavy dose of negative skepticism... all of which was quickly abandoned with my first bite. The buttery richness overtook my palate, the creamy flavors fixated my senses, and 1 was immersed in an edible experience that has since been the focus of all daydreams and edible fantasies.

98
Hana Farms
Wood-Fired
Pizza Night

While this farm/gift-stand is best known for their banana bread, preserves, and coffee—the real treat is their farm-to-table pizza night. They hand toss dough, top it with whatever is growing around the farm, then wood fire it in their clay oven—and if you order to-go, they wrap it in a banana leaf! Best of all, this night (usually on the weekends) has become a high-energy social gathering for the Hana area, making it a great place for locals and tourists of all ages to come share the aloha spirit.

99
Ono Organic Farms
Maui-Grown Cacao Beans

The Boerner's family farm was rockin' organic decades before it became trendy, and still crank out the same "Ono-licious" products today. All of these different fruits—more than you knew existed— are handpicked and available for purchase at their stand in Hana town, along with the coffee and cacao (chocolate) beans that they grow and roast themselves! If you're looking to do more than gorge at their stand, check out the deliciously educational tours and tastings they offer.

100
Hana's
Dish of the Day

Unfortunately, the food inconsistency in the Hana area makes it impractical for me to pick a specific lunch dish or even a certain eatery. However, despite never knowing for sure who will be open, there is always something delicious being served. Maybe you'll get lucky and Pranee will be dishing up her famous Mahi Mahi curry, or perhaps you'll find the Huli Huli Chicken guys are roasting away down on the beach— whatever the case, forget that boring sack lunch from Paia. Follow your nose or just ask some locals... you'll be sure to find something #DroolWorthy.

101
Bonus

Spot:

Item:

What's it all
Take a photo and share with the rest of us!
#MauiFoodist

102
Bonus

Spot:

Item:

> *What's it all*
>
>
>
>
>
>
>
>
>
>
>
>
> *Take a photo and share with the rest of us!*
> *#MauiFoodist*

Names & Notes

Names & Notes

One Last Thing...

I worked hard to make this a list that turns the volume on your Maui experience up to 11, doesn't waste your time, and leaves you feeling like you had some uniquely awesome experiences.

If I was successful, I would truly appreciate if you help spread the word via social media...

#MauiFoodist

If I didn't live up to your expectations, e-mail:

Marjerison@gmail.com

So I can make it better.

/MauiFoodist

 @MauiFoodist

 @MauiFoodist

MauiFoodist.com

Iver Marjerison

Since first biting into a fresh pineapple on a family trip when he was just 6 years old, Iver has been infatuated by the magical tastes of Maui. Post graduation, he has gone on to get his MBA in Sustainable Food Systems, and works as a writer, educator, and marketing consultant through his company **Food Flow**. *While his passion is to help improve the sustainability of our global food system, he often—and gleefully—gets sidetracked hunting down and sharing edible adventures.*

He currently resides in his truck bed camper, parked wherever his food-obsessed imagination has most recently been captured.

IverMarjerison.com Marjerison@gmail.com

CPSIA information can be obtained
at www.ICGtesting.com
Printed in the USA
BVHW080318121121
621442BV00008B/333

9 780578 580418